Build Your Network
How to Create a World-Class Social Circle

Disclaimer

All attempts have been made to verify the information in this book; however, neither the author nor the publisher assumes any responsibility for errors, omissions, or contrary interpretations of the content within.

This book is for entertainment purposes only, and so the views of the author should not be taken as expert instruction or commands. The reader is responsible for his or her own actions.

This book is not meant to be used, nor should it be used, to diagnose or treat any medical condition. For diagnosis or treatment of any medical problem, consult your own physician.

The people described in this book are real, but their names and circumstances have been changed to protect the confidentiality of each individual.

Neither the author nor the publisher assumes any responsibility or liability on behalf of the purchaser or reader of this book.

Buyer Bonus

As a way of saying thank you for your purchase, I'm offering a *free* download for my book readers.

I created a cheat sheet that will help you approach and talk to anybody.

>>> Go to

www.socialconfidencemastery.com/cheatsheet

Inside, you will learn how to do the following:

- change your mindset by training your mind to improve the way you see yourself

- create a killer first impression and become a more likable person right away

- overcome social anxiety by building your courage to approach anybody you want to meet

- improve your conversation skills by learning how to tell good stories that captivate people

- design your ideal lifestyle by doing more of what you love while connecting with like-minded people

… and much, much more.

Dedication

This book is dedicated to all my previous students. You are the reason why I do what I do. I am honored to play a small role in your social success.

I also want to dedicate this book to my family, which has supported my unconventional journey thus far. Mom, Dad, Carlo, Jean—thank you for believing in me.

Let's not forget my friends who have inspired me to keep going during tough moments. Deon, Joe, Rachael, and Patrick—I'm grateful for your support.

Table of Contents

Chapter 1: Why Your Network Is Your Biggest Asset in Life 2

Chapter 2: How to Meet the Right People 7

Chapter 3: Networking Mistakes to Avoid at All Cost 12

Chapter 4: 5 Tips to Overcome Your Shyness 17

Chapter 5: How to Develop Your Courage to Meet People 22

Chapter 6: Why Looks Matter More Than You Think 26

Chapter 7: How to Build Rapport Instantly 30

Chapter 8: How to Improve Your Conversation Skills 35

Chapter 9: What to Talk About in Conversation 39

Chapter 10: How to Connect with Influential People 42

Chapter 11: Where to Meet More Like-Minded People 46

Chapter 12: How to Socialize with Ease 51

Chapter 13: The Fastest Way to Grow Your Network 55

Chapter 14: How to Live a Life That Excites You .. 59

Chapter 15: How to Become a People Magnet 62

How to Use This Book

Here's the reality of your situation: anyone can pick up and read this book—but not everyone will see results.

The difference between the guy who improves his social confidence and the guy who just buys another book on social confidence is one simple thing: taking massive action.

If you want to get the most out of this book, I encourage you to do three things:

1. Have an open mind so you can accept new ideas.

2. Implement the strategies that you learn as you're reading.

3. Take what works and discard what doesn't.

These are the same steps that I took to change my own life and the lives of the clients I've worked with through my coaching program.

You can't just read a book and expect to get results. You need to apply what you learn consistently until it works for you.

That's why I've made this book actionable.

If you do this, I promise you that your personal, romantic, and professional lives will transform and you'll start becoming the man you've always wanted to be.

Chapter 1
Why Your Network Is Your Biggest Asset in Life

Imagine how meeting higher-caliber people, creating meaningful relationships faster, and doubling the size of your network would impact every aspect of your life.

Technology is supposed to improve our connection with other people, but it's actually causing us to be more socially isolated. More and more people are losing their ability to engage and connect with those around them because they're spending too much time with their smartphones and on social media.

Don't get me wrong: I'm all for leveraging technology, and in a lot of ways, it has made my life better. But if you want more opportunities in your personal and professional life, you need to learn how to engage people in real life.

Smartphones and social media should be used to enhance your existing relationships and build your network; it's not a replacement for face-to-face interactions.

I know this from experience.

Throughout the years, I've had incredible things happen to me because I knew how to connect with people online and offline.

Here are a few examples. I've been able to quit my corporate job and build a successful consulting business. I've also appeared on national television multiple times, and I regularly get invited to exclusive events with all my expenses paid for. I have friends from all over the world, and I can't remember the last time I had to pay for a hotel.

I'm not saying those things to brag; I'm saying them to show you what's possible if you know how to build your network.

But it hasn't always been that way for me.

My family and I moved to Canada when I was 16 years old. Initially, I struggled connecting with people because I didn't speak English and suffered from really bad social anxiety.

In fact, I was stuck working low-paying jobs for many years because I had low self-esteem and couldn't communicate effectively.

As I looked around me, I noticed other people who had the lifestyle I wanted. They exuded confidence, did meaningful work, and had lots of friends.

They were cool and popular, and I wanted to be just like them. The only problem was that I had no clue where to even begin.

Frustrated with my situation, I was determined to make a change. I knew I had to do something different and figure out this part of my life.

For many years, I read every book about social dynamics I could get my hands on. I went out of my way to learn from some of the best in this industry, and I also experimented on my own.

Things were hard, but I didn't quit. I had no choice but to succeed. I could either figure this out or spend the rest of my life lonely and depressed.

After many years of hard work and persistence, this whole thing finally made sense.

My life has changed dramatically since I learned how to improve my social confidence.

That's why I wrote this book. I wanted to share with you the lessons I've learned so you can also build a thriving social circle in today's world. Whatever you're trying to achieve in your life, having a quality network is your best asset.

My experience reminds me of James, a former student of mine.

When James reached out to me, he'd just left a horrible marriage. He was a single dad and worked as an engineer.

James got married and had a kid at a young age. Having a demanding career and supporting a family didn't leave him a lot of time to do anything else. He never had much of a social life outside of work.

When he came to me, he was newly single and didn't have any friends. He wanted to go out and meet new people, but he had no idea where to even begin.

During the coaching program, I taught James how to become a people magnet and build quality relationships with like-minded people.

Last time I talked to James, he'd been promoted at work, moved to a new city to start a new life, and made new friends. He was also actively going on dates again and connecting with quality women.

If you're not a naturally social person, don't worry. Just like any skill, building your network can be learned with the right knowledge, practice, and repetition.

If you follow the lessons in this book, I promise that you, too, can surround yourself with the type of people you want to meet.

What you'll learn from this book has been proven to work in real-life situations. It's not only practical; it's also very applicable.

With great success, I implemented the lessons in this book before I taught it to my coaching clients. My hope is that it changes your life the same way it changed ours.

If you're ready to build a quality network, then don't delay any longer.

Let's jump right in.

Chapter 2

How to Meet the Right People

Before anything else, I want to share with you one of my favorite quotes by Stephen Covey:

"To begin with the end in mind means to start with a clear understanding of your destination. It means to know where you're going so that you better understand where you are now and so that the steps you take are always in the right direction."

So before you start building your network, you have to figure out what kind of relationships you want to have in the first place.

Keep in mind that you become the average of the people you spend the most time with, so be intentional about the social circle you create.

That's why it's so important to have a clearly defined goal.

Knowing what you want acts like a filter and helps you make decisions faster. You'll be able to reach your destination faster with less stress and frustration.

Let's take Rick, one of my previous coaching clients, as an example.

Rick works as a computer programmer and is extremely introverted, which means he doesn't have a lot of energy when it comes to meeting new people.

When he reached out to me, he was extremely frustrated with his dating and social life. He barely had any friends, and he went on a lot of awkward first dates.

When we started working together, the first thing I asked him to do was define his core values and the things that matter to him.

This is important because mutual interests are the foundation of every great relationship. It's so much easier to spend time with people who like the same things you do.

It took a while for Rick to identify what he wanted, but the time he invested figuring it out was definitely worth it. Once he got clear about his ideal dating and social life, I held him accountable throughout the coaching program so that every decision he made supported his goal.

Because he was aware about what he valued, it was easy for him to start going to places where the type of people he wanted to meet would also hang out.

In just a few weeks, he made a lot of new friends and met a girl who ended up becoming his girlfriend.

Last time I talked to him, they were still dating and he'd filled his network with like-minded individuals.

Rick was able to accomplish his goal quickly because his efforts were focused.

Can you see how powerful this is?

So before you move forward to the next chapter, I want you to identify the things that are important to you and the kinds of relationships you want in your life.

I'm encouraging you to give your goal a lot of thought. The preparation you do up front will help you connect with the right people very quickly.

To give you an example from my own life, I wanted to be around other people who value doing meaningful work, love personal development, and live a healthy lifestyle.

I made a list of places and activities these people would be into, and I picked which ones I liked to do as well.

That's why I don't spend as much time going to bars and nightclubs. Those types of venues attract lots of younger people who like to party, which is definitely not my crowd.

Nowadays, I spend a lot of time at coffee shops, coworking spaces, personal development seminars, gyms, and fitness classes. The people I want to meet are already there, and I enjoy doing those things, too.

Another thing I want you to ask yourself is why it's important for you to achieve your goal.

Everything is hard at first, and it's easy to make excuses when the going gets tough. Trust me when I say you're a lot more likely to achieve your goals if you have a strong emotional reason behind it.

For me, it wasn't hard to find my motivation to improve my social confidence and put myself out there. I hated my job, I barely had friends, and my dating life was nonexistent. I was already in so much pain back then that I was willing to do whatever I had to do.

I never wanted to feel lonely again.

I can't be the guy who keeps watching other people have fun while I stand on the sidelines nursing my drink. I wanted to express who I truly am without worrying what other people might think.

I was tired of seeing beautiful girls and feeling helpless because I didn't know what to do.

I wanted to feel empowered and in control of who I met. I wanted quality people to include me in their plans instead of always being left out.

The pain of not doing anything was greater than making a change, but the emotional connection I had with my goal kept me going when I was ready to quit.

Whatever your goal is, you need to attach a strong feeling to it. Use pain as a motivator to propel you forward.

Again, make sure you have clearly defined goals and that you know why they matter to you before moving on to the next chapter.

Chapter 3

Networking Mistakes to Avoid at All Cost

You already know that having a quality network is crucial to your personal and professional success.

But if you are making these networking mistakes, then you might be rubbing people the wrong way without you knowing it.

Learning how to build relationships with people is a process, and it definitely takes time. I've made all these mistakes, and I've also seen my students do the same thing, so pay close attention.

Here they are.

Mistake #1: Not Being Specific

We're all given the same amount of time every single day. That's why you have to be careful with how you spend it.

Like I said earlier, being specific about the type of people you want to meet is crucial. Having a goal will help you make the right decisions about where to go and who to build relationships with.

If you don't know where you're going, any map will take you there, so make sure you have a clearly defined goal.

Mistake #2: Not Meeting Enough People

When guys come to me for help, one of the first things I asked them is to describe their social lives. I need to know what they're currently doing to build their network.

Most of them are shy, don't have a lot of experience meeting new people, and have the same boring weekly routine of just doing the same things over and over again.

This reminds me of Jim, one of my previous students.

Jim works as a mechanical engineer. When he reached out to me, he's been lonely for so long that was ready to make a change He wanted to learn how to meet new people and take control of his dating and social life.

During the coaching program, I explained to him that social confidence is a muscle that gets stronger the more he used it. It's no different than going to the gym. The more you work out, the more fit you are. The more people you talk to, the faster you improve socially.

I hate to break it to you, but if all you do is go to work, go home, watch Netflix, and play video games every week, it's going to be hard to grow your network. It is a number's game, after all.

The more people you meet, the more opportunities you create. Treat this as an important part of your personal development.

Accept all valid invitations from people. Avoid staying at home, and make it a point to go to at least a few social events on a weekly basis.

I'll go through this in much greater detail later on in the book.

Mistake #3: Not Following Up

Most people I've worked with give up way too early.

Just because you didn't hear back from someone you're trying to connect with doesn't mean they're not interested.

For me, I get busy and forget to respond sometimes. Life happens, and you don't know what's going on in people's lives. That's why it's important to keep following up.

If you want to build a quality network, you need to be patient and persistent. I encourage you to make a list of important people you want to keep in touch with. Set a reminder to send them a thoughtful message at least every couple of weeks.

It could be a text or a phone call. Or you could just hit them up on social media to show that they crossed your mind. Thoughtfulness does go a long way.

Mistake #4: Poor Presentation

You never get a second chance to make a good first impression.

If you want people to get to know you, you have to look like a person of value.

You might be a great guy, but if you're poorly dressed and not well groomed, the people you meet might get the wrong impression of you.

The way you look should bridge the gap between how you see yourself and how you want other people to see you. That's why you need to put some effort into your overall presentation.

You can influence how others perceive you through your style, grooming, and body language, so you need to take this seriously.

I'll give you more tips on how to do this later on in the book.

Mistake #5: Asking for More Than You Give

A relationship is like a plant: it takes time to grow and you can't rush it.

Don't be that guy who only calls people when you need something. That's really annoying, and if you keep doing that, people will stop being in contact with you.

Give more than you take and nurture your relationships. Treat your network like your bank account. You want to deposit more than you withdraw.

There you have it. These are the most common networking mistakes that I've seen and that I've committed as well. Avoid them at all cost.

Chapter 4

5 Tips to Overcome Your Shyness

Being shy can hold you back from meeting new people and building a thriving social circle.

cane Iidnere Interacting with a total stranger can feel very uncomfortable, especially if you don't have a lot of experience doing it. The fear of rejection or being judged by others can be paralyzing as well.

If you don't know how to manage your insecurities, it can cause you to isolate yourself and avoid social situations. Eventually, this can lead to feelings of loneliness and depression.

As someone who used to be extremely shy, I was stuck at home every weekend because I had no friends. On the rare occasion I'd actually be invited to a party, I felt too anxious to mingle with the people around me.

I found it hard to just be myself, and I was always stuck in my head and worried what others might be thinking of me.

Can you relate to this?

If so, I want to share with you a few things I've learned that helped me overcome my shyness

Here are my best tips.

Tip #1: Appreciate Yourself

Comparing yourself to other people is a quick way to feel like you're not good enough.

If you want to feel more confident about who you are, go out of your way to find things you like about yourself. This is one of the best ways to increase your self-worth.

For example, I used to be very insecure about my height and my ethnicity. I was afraid people wouldn't like me because I was short and looked different than everybody else.

It wasn't until I started to appreciate my other positive traits that I started to really like who I was, regardless of my race and physical stature.

You'll get exactly what you focus on, so the more aware you are of your positive traits, the better you'll feel about yourself.

Tip #2: Pick Your Battles

Your social value is relative to your environment.

If you consider yourself a more reserved and sensitive person, you should stay away from extremely loud places, where you won't be able to display your positive traits.

Put yourself in situations where you have a better chance of success. That's why it's so important to spend more time meeting people while doing things you enjoy.

Even if you don't meet anyone while you're there, you'll still have fun because you'll be doing something you like.

For example, I have a lot of knowledge and experience in sales and marketing. My expertise will be a lot more appreciated at a networking event full of entrepreneurs than a nightclub with drunk people who hate their jobs.

Take the time to figure out what your strengths are. Know what you're good at and play games you can win.

Tip #3: Shift Your Focus

In life, there are things that are permanent and there are things you can change. The feeling of anxiety comes from trying to control things that you can't.

Your job is to accept the things you can't do anything about and shift your focus to things you can control.

You can't predict how people will respond to you when you meet them. But you can put more effort into improving your mindset, dressing well, and pursuing your passion.

Do what you can and let go of the rest. Trust me, you'll feel a lot better and less stressed in any social setting.

Tip #4: Share Your Interests

Have you ever talked to someone who's so passionate about what they do?

It's very captivating, isn't it?

It's not really the thing you talk about that people find interesting. It's the fact that you're actually passionate about something.

Whatever you're into, there's always someone out there who would like the same things as you. That's why you should always talk about your passion.

Sharing your interests also qualifies the people that you meet. You can find out very quickly if you have things in common or not.

Tip #5: Cut Your Losses

Believe it or not, you should be thankful every time you get rejected.

The same way you don't like everyone you meet, not everybody you meet is going to like you. That's why the faster you disqualify people who are not a good fit, the faster you'll meet the right people.

Besides, why would you want to hang out with people who don't like you, anyway?

That's really it. Implement these tips on a regular basis and you'll eventually be able to overcome your shyness.

Chapter 5

How to Develop Your Courage to Meet People

Nothing great ever comes from playing it safe.

If you want an exciting life, you need to learn how to take risks. Otherwise, you'll end up with a lot of regrets and resentments.

Being afraid of the unknown is totally normal.

But the question is, are you going to let that feeling stop you from living a more fulfilling life, or are you going to feel the fear and act anyway?

Fear is just an emotional reaction to an unfamiliar situation. The funny thing is, as soon as you change the story you tell yourself, you also change how you feel at that moment.

If you're anything like I was back in the day, I'm sure you could come up with a lot of reasons why people wouldn't like you.

These were some of the bullshit stories I used to tell myself:

"I'm too short."

"I'm not fit enough."

"I'm not well dressed."

"People don't like Asians."

"I have nothing good to say."

Blah. Blah. Blah.

If you want to succeed socially and build your network, be mindful of what you focus on.

Can you come up with just one reason why you would be successful? I'm sure you can.

Now I want you to put all your focus and energy onto supporting that thought and to make all your decisions from that place.

Whatever you're afraid of, I want you to ask yourself this question: "What's the worst-case scenario?"

After working with dozens and dozens of clients in the past, I discovered that most of them have an unrealistic and exaggerated version of what failure looks like.

This reminds me of Mark, one of my previous coaching clients.

Mark is a professional engineer. When he came to me, he had no social life and seriously hadn't gone on a date with any woman in over a decade!

When I asked him why, his answer blew me away.

Back when he was in university, he asked a girl he liked to go see a movie with him. Unfortunately, she wasn't interested, and she politely turned him down.

Mark took that rejection so personally it prevented him from meeting new people and putting himself out there for a long time. When we started working together, he actually believed that women would spit at him if he showed any romantic interest.

If you can relate to Mark, I want you to know that you're not alone. That's why I want you to question the stories you tell yourself, because they may or may not be true.

Assuming you're not being weird and disrespectful, you're not going to experience any harsh rejections. I've literally met thousands of new people, and not once do I remember anyone treating me poorly, let alone spitting at me.

The next question I want you to ask yourself is this: "What's the best-case scenario?"

It's funny how most guys don't even think about this. In every interaction, things can go well or not. Both are possible, and that's just how life works.

But most guys I've worked with only focus on things going bad. What if things actually worked out?

To give you a few examples from my personal life, I've dated amazing women I met while sitting at a coffee shop. I've been asked to speak on stage because I said hello to someone who knew the organizer. I've appeared on national television numerous times because I randomly met someone who knew the producer.

None of those things would've happened if I hadn't taken a risk and courageously put myself out there.

Also, you can't take rejection personally.

You don't know what people are going through. Maybe their boss yelled at them earlier that day. Maybe they just failed an exam. Or maybe they're just not that into you.

Who knows? Your guess is as good as mine.

Remember, time is your most valuable asset, so don't waste it with the wrong people.

Like I said earlier, your job is to filter out those who are not interested in you and move on. There are billions of people out there. Choose those who choose you back.

Chapter 6

Why Looks Matter More Than You Think

I usually shake my head when I hear people say that dressing well is either feminine or superficial.

They argue that it's what's on the inside that matters most. Better yet, people should really take the time to get to know their personality.

You know what? I totally agree. If you have a terrible personality, it doesn't matter how well dressed you are.

But the thing is, if you want others to take the time to get to know you, you have to look like someone worth getting to know.

That makes sense, right?

Let's take John, one of my previous coaching clients, as an example.

Even though John was a well-educated dentist, he struggled to build his clientele and get dates with women.

When he came to me for help, I could see what the problem was.

John had bad posture, was poorly groomed, and wore ill-fitting clothes.

When he implemented the lessons I'm about to share with you, he was able to put together an attractive and still very professional image. He was also able to improve his charisma and portray himself as an authority in his industry.

Last time I talked to him, his clinic was a lot busier and he was regularly going on more dates.

The thing is, it didn't matter how qualified or educated John was as a dentist. Because he didn't present himself properly, not many people cared.

Here's the truth: looks do matter!

If you see someone with good style, what would you think? You might assume he's successful and has his life together.

Now, if you see the same guy wearing dirty and ill-fitting clothes, you'd probably think he's a slob and that his life is going nowhere.

People are going to judge you no matter what, so you might as well take advantage of it.

Your style introduces you before you even say a word. Think of it like your personal brand.

Your body can only change so much through eating healthy and working out, but you can always do something about what you wear.

Also, upgrading your style is the quickest way to improve your self-image. You can transform yourself from someone who looks very average into someone who people pay attention to and respect.

All it takes is a basic, fundamental understanding of style and grooming.

I hope by now I've convinced you that dressing well is something you need to take seriously.

If you're not sure where to start, it's not that hard.

Just think of someone who's already attracting the type of people you want to meet. What do they seem to wear?

Do a bit of research online and make a list of clothing items you need to buy.

To give you an example, I wanted people to think I was intriguing and a bit of a badass. I wanted to attract highly motivated and creative people in my life.

When I started looking more into changing the way I dressed, I resonated with Lewis Howes; he's a best-selling author, a podcast host, and a very successful lifestyle entrepreneur.

I paid attention to what he was wearing and how he presented himself. I noticed that he wore a lot of dark colors, minimal patterns, and leather jackets.

He looked intriguing and definitely badass.

So what did I do?

I started investing in those same clothing items until I found my own style. Emulate before you innovate.

Dressing well doesn't have to be complicated. All you have to do is to figure out what's already working and make it your own.

Chapter 7
How to Build Rapport Instantly

If you want to rapidly grow your network, you need to learn how to turn strangers into friends right away.

Building rapport with people I just met definitely wasn't a skill I had when I was younger. Because I was so socially awkward, I avoided interacting with others as much possible and would just keep to myself.

After many years of consciously working on this part of my life, I've learned a few important lessons that helped me improve my social confidence.

Nowadays, I feel a lot more comfortable going to parties and networking events and even traveling on my own. This is because I know I can handle myself comfortably and with great success in a variety of social situations.

If only I'd known these things back in the day, my life would've been completely different today.

That's why I want to share these tips with you.

Here they are.

Tip #1: Be Interested

In order to come across as an interesting person, you need to be interested in other people first.

This is the most important thing you need to remember if you want to win someone over very quickly.

People love talking about themselves, so go ahead and let them. Encourage them to share, and give them the spotlight.

If you do that, the other person will leave that interaction feeling heard and understood, even if you didn't get to talk much.

Tip #2: Give a Genuine Compliment

As Dale Carnegie would say, "Be hearty in your approbation and lavish in your praise."

One of the best ways I know to start a conversation is to give a genuine compliment. Train yourself to look for things that are worth praising in other people.

Also, if you want your compliment to sound more authentic, be more specific. Instead of saying "I like your shirt," say "You have such good style. Tell me how you put together that outfit."

This will make your compliments more memorable to the person receiving them.

Tip #3: Explore Mutual Interests

Have you ever met someone who you instantly clicked with? It's probably because you had a lot of things in common.

Familiarity builds comfort very quickly, so explore as many mutual interests as you can. Make it easy for people to talk to you by volunteering information about yourself as well.

For example, work is a pretty common thing to talk about.

When someone asks you what you do, instead of just saying "I'm an engineer," you can say "I work as a software engineer for a startup and I went to school in Vancouver. While I was there, I developed a passion for yoga as well because all my friends were doing it."

Do you see how much better that sounds? The more details you share, the faster you'll be able to find commonality with everyone you talk to.

Tip #4: Ask Good Questions

If you've ever been stuck making small talk, there's a good chance you were asking closed-ended questions that could be answered with yes or no.

To improve the quality of your interactions, learn to ask more open-ended questions.

For example, instead of asking "Do you like your job?" ask "What do you like most about your job?" Open-ended questions keep the conversation flowing and are much more engaging.

This also encourages the person you're talking to share more information about themselves, which will help you find more things to talk about.

Tip #5: Listen to Understand

Everybody wants to feel heard and understood.

If you want to build rapport with people right away, you have to be a good listener. Give the person you're talking to your full, undivided attention, and pay attention to what they're saying instead of just listening to reply.

You'll never have to worry about running out of things to say if you're fully present in your conversations. The right response will come to you if you're just in the moment.

Tip #6: Read Between the Lines

A big part of your communication is nonverbal. There's more to what people say than just the words coming out of their mouths.

That's why it's so important to be empathetic. Make an effort to see things from other people's perspectives, and put yourself in their shoes.

By doing this, you'll be able to communicate with more compassion and deepen your connection with everyone you talk to.

Tip #7: Make Eye Contact

It's hard to be perceived as someone trustworthy if you don't look people in the eye. Make sure you maintain proper eye contact when talking to people.

I know it can feel a little bit uncomfortable, so make a game out of it. Next time you interact with someone, look them in the eye long enough to remember their eye color.

Tip #8: Smile

There's nothing more inviting than a genuine smile.

It signals to other people that you're happy and in a good mood. Even if you're not feeling that great, forcing yourself to smile will immediately make you feel better. Your physiology affects your psychology.

Say "cookies" underneath your breath, and you'll project a genuine smile.

I know I've given you lots of things to work on, so be patient.

Consistently implementing these tips might take some time and practice, but if you keep at it, you'll be able to get people you just met to like you right away.

Chapter 8

How to Improve Your Conversation Skills

Learning how to hold an interesting conversation is a skill worth its weight in gold.

If you want to succeed at building a quality network, you need to communicate your ideas effectively.

This reminds me of Kyle, one of my previous students.

Kyle immigrated to Canada from the Philippines when he was young, and now he works as an engineer.

His parents really pushed the idea of academic success as his ticket to everything he wanted in life. He devoted all his time to studying and getting good grades so he could land a high-paying job.

When he reached out to me, he was really struggling socially. He always caught himself in a lot of awkward situations simply because he barely had any experience interacting with people.

Because he applied all the tips I'm about to share with you, he was able to improve his conversations skills very rapidly.

If you want to learn how to improve your connection with everyone you talk to, here are my best tips.

Tip #1: Talk More Slowly

Most shy people can't stand awkward silences in conversation, so they compensate by talking too fast.

This becomes an issue when others have to keep asking you to repeat what you just said because they can't understand you.

A good way to calm yourself when you're feeling nervous is to just breathe slowly. Doing this will get you out of your head and put you back in the moment. Now you can gather your ideas more clearly and communicate them better.

Tip #2: Make More Statements

Asking questions when you meet someone for the first time is necessary. It allows you gather information, which can help you decided which way you want to steer the conversation.

It's when you repeatedly ask questions and don't share anything about yourself that it starts to feel intrusive. It creates zero rapport, so avoid doing this at all cost.

The next time you're talking to someone, make sure there's an equal balance of sharing and relating. For example, when someone tells you what they do for work, talk a little bit about what you do as well before asking another question.

Another thing you can do is make more observations. For example, instead of saying "Where are you from?"

you can try to say "Your style looks like you'd be from the East Coast. Are you from Toronto by any chance?" This sounds way more interesting because people love learning about themselves.

Tip #3: Open Up

Your body language plays a huge role in the way you convey your ideas. That's why it's so important to pay attention to your nonverbal communication.

If you want to look more approachable, always remember to smile and have your arms on your side. Having a frown on your face with your arms crossed doesn't look very inviting.

Most of the guys I've worked with in the past have desk jobs. They sit in front of a computer all day, which gives them a hunched look.

If that sounds like you, there's a way you can fix your posture almost instantly. All you have to do is stand against the wall and make sure the back of your head, the back of your shoulders, your butt, and your heels all touch the wall.

Tip # 4: Relate Emotionally

One of the biggest mistakes I see shy guys make in conversation is talking too logically.

Facts and data are good if you're delivering your quarterly report to your boss, but not so much if you want to be an engaging conversationalist.

If you don't want to bore people to death, add some emotions into your stories. Tell them how things made you feel. Also, be more descriptive by talking about what you saw, what you heard, what you smelled, what you felt, and what you tasted.

Relating emotionally and engaging the senses will make your stories way more interesting.

Tip # 5: Be Vulnerable

People relate through struggles, so don't be afraid to share some personal stuff in conversation.

Talk about things you had troubles with and how you overcame them. By doing this, you're providing a safe space for the other person to open up as well, which creates a deeper connection.

If you're not a naturally social person, implement these tips and you'll improve your conversation skills in no time.

Chapter 9
What to Talk About in Conversation

Having awkward silences in conversations has to be one of the biggest struggles most of my coaching clients have.

But if you think about it, it's actually impossible to run out of things to say. You have decades of life experiences that you can share in conversation.

Just in case you're still lost and not sure where to start, I have a few suggestions to help you get started.

Here are some potential conversation topics.

Topic #1: Your Hobbies

Talking about your hobby is great because you know a lot about it.

Not only that, but once you get good at something, you can use that same skill to relate and create parallels when you're talking about an unfamiliar topic.

Topic #2: Your Passions

Like I said before, passion is sexy because it gives your life a sense of direction. It's easy to get out of bed when you're excited about how you're going to spend your day.

Not only that, but having something you're working toward becomes a source of internal happiness. This helps eliminate neediness and desperation.

This point is so important that you'll hear me mention it all throughout the book.

Topic #3: Your Upbringing

The way you were brought up has a huge influence on how you turn out.

I find it easier to connect with someone who shares similar family values, so make sure you bring those up in conversation whenever you can.

Topic #4: Places You've Been To

Traveling has to be one of the best things anyone can do.

It helps you become more empathetic because you get to have a wide range of life experiences.

Not only that, but you have an opportunity to learn a lot about who you are by putting yourself through different situations.

Save your money by not buying useless crap, and make it a point to travel more often.

Tip #5: Events You've Attended

There's no way around it.

If you want to be an interesting conversationalist, you need to do more interesting things.

It's hard to be good in conversation if all you do is go to work, go home, and hang out with the same people over the weekend.

You have to go out and do more things.

A good way to get started is to go to personal development retreats, a seminar about a topic you want to learn, or an industry-related conference.

Don't feel overwhelmed and like you have to do all these things at once. It's just something you want to keep in mind and work toward.

I hope these topic suggestions help you out in conversation.

Also, make sure you craft these stories ahead of time.

You wouldn't write an exam you didn't study for, right? So if you're not a naturally good storyteller, then make sure you prepare what you want to talk about before you go out.

I recommended you handwrite these stories so you remember them better. When you know what you want to talk about, you'll feel a lot more confident interacting with anybody anywhere you go.

Remember, preparation breeds confidence.

Chapter 10

How to Connect with Influential People

Before I learned how to connect with the right people, I was in a bad situation. I was broke, hated my job, and barely had friends. My life was unfulfilling, and I had no idea how to change it.

Like I said earlier, I've had a lot of amazing things happen to my life because I have relationships with prominent individuals. Not only do they know other influential people, but they also have information that can quickly get you where you want to go.

If you want to have more opportunities in your life, you need to know how to connect with the right people.

Here's how to get started.

Tip #1: Get Noticed

Most influencers nowadays have some sort of presence online. Look them up and get to know them on a personal level.

Pay attention to what they're posting and engage with their content.

For example, you can visit their website and buy their books on Amazon. Subscribe to their newsletter and check out their blog.

Watch their videos on YouTube and listen to their podcasts. Like their page on Facebook and follow them on LinkedIn. Retweet them on Twitter and engage with their photos on Instagram.

If you do this authentically and repeatedly, they'll start to notice you and pay attention to you as well.

Tip #2: Reach Out

If you did your homework in advance, this one should be fairly easy.

Because you've familiarized yourself with an influencer's content, you can be more thoughtful with your outreach instead of being generic.

Based on your research, pick something specific you can relate to and message them about it.

Maybe both of you are from the same hometown. Or maybe both of you enjoy playing a specific sport. It could even be your taste in music or your favorite food.

Like I said earlier, familiarity builds comfort, so find as much commonality as you can. Choose something that stands out to you and go from there.

Tip #3: Share Your Results

The fastest way to connect with any influencer is to take their advice, put it into action, and let them know about your results.

Doesn't it feel good when you know people listen to what you have to say? Not only will influencers notice you, but they also will want to help you more and connect you to their network, too.

For example, back in the day I took a course that helped me start my online business. I applied all the lessons I learned and was able to quit my job and work from anywhere after only a few months.

I emailed the course creators about my results, and they promoted the crap out of me to their audience. We also became good friends and developed a personal relationship.

Talk is cheap. Those people who walk the walk are the ones who get noticed by influencers.

Tip #4: Help Them Out

It's rare to find an influential person who's well rounded. Because they've invested all their time mastering their craft, there's a good chance they've neglected other areas of their life.

They might be struggling with something you're good at.

That's when you come into the picture.

For example, I've gone to the gym with a few of my mentors because they wanted to learn how to work out.

I've even taken some of them shopping because they were about to speak on stage.

If you want to become memorable, find opportunities to help influential people solve one of their pressing problems.

Tip #5: Be Normal

Influential people are obviously popular.

They have fans that adore and look up to them. Because they have something that others don't, people always want to get something from them.

Don't be like that.

Treat them like a regular person and connect with them on a deeper level. Be interested in who they are as a person, not just in their accomplishments.

That's how you position yourself as a friend, not as a fan.

These are the exact things I did to connect with influential people. Apply these tips regularly and you'll be able to network your way to a better lifestyle and a higher net worth.

Chapter 11
Where to Meet More Like-Minded People

As you've learned so far in this book, who you keep close says a lot about who you are.

You become the average of the people you spend the most time with.

I wish I knew this when I was in my early twenties. My life today would've been completely different.

Back then, I was insecure, unsuccessful, and going nowhere in life. Knowing what I know now, it was no coincidence.

The people I was around were mostly living paycheck to paycheck. All they wanted to do was go out, get drunk, and chase after girls.

It took me long enough to realize how pointless that was. That's when I decided to trade my old friends for new ones.

You have to be mindful of who you're around all the time. Their beliefs and habits will eventually rub off on you.

Think of the type of people you want to meet and ask yourself where they hang out. As the saying goes, 80% of success is just showing up, but you have to show up at the right places.

You're a lot more likely to accomplish your goals if you're with people who have what you want. Your social circle is your source of inspiration and motivation.

Here are the best places I recommend meeting more like-minded people.

Tip #1: Join a Meetup Group

Meetup is an online resource that can help you meet new people.

You can find a group of people interested in a particular subject for almost every topic you can think of.

Sign up for a free account and pick the things you're interested in. Meetup will show you upcoming events related to whatever you're into, and you can also see who's attending.

Once you're there, starting a conversation with anyone you want to meet is easy because a common interest brought both of you together.

Tip #2: Organize Your Own Events

At any party, the host always has the highest social value, so make sure you organize your own events.

Invite your closest friends and interesting people you've met throughout the week. Be proactive about growing your network by telling whoever is coming to bring new people, too. If you get along with your current social circle, chances are they can introduce you to someone you'll like as well.

A bit of creativity goes a long way. You can organize barbecues at a park, a hike on a nice day, or a dinner party at a restaurant.

This is one of the best ways I've built my network whenever I moved to a new city. I highly recommend you give this a shot.

Tip #3: Learn a New Skill

If you want to become an interesting person, you need to do interesting things.

Ask yourself what skill or hobby you've always wanted to learn.

Whether it's learning Spanish, playing the guitar, or dabbling with photography, go ahead and give it a shot.

Not only will you become a more well-rounded person, but you'll also have a more diverse group of friends.

Tip #4: Attend Relevant Conferences

It's sad that most people don't think twice when buying new clothes or the latest iPhone but that they hesitate when it comes to investing in personal development.

In every aspect of your life, you are the common denominator. How you do one thing is how you do everything.

That's why *you* are your best asset.

If you're the type of guy who's also looking for other growth-minded people, you'll definitely find them at conferences and seminars.

Pick a topic you want to learn more about and sign up. A paid event is also a good way to meet higher-quality individuals because they are serious about being there.

Whether it's a professional or personal development event, you're guaranteed to walk away with not just a new idea but also a great connection.

Tip #5: Leverage Social Media

Social media has revolutionized how we interact with each other, and it's become an integral part of how we connect with people.

You can literally access thousands of potential connections just by using your smartphone.

All you have to do is find relevant groups on your preferred social media platform. Start off by introducing yourself and then join the existing conversation in the group by asking questions or commenting on the existing threads.

Leverage the power of social media to find like-minded people more quickly. Once you've found some people you think you'll get along with, exchange contact information and meet each other offline.

There you have it. These are my best tips to meet more like-minded people. I've applied them with great success in my own life, and so have my coaching clients.

I know I gave you a lot of stuff to work with, so just pick the easiest one that you can implement right away.

Chapter 12
How to Socialize with Ease

Will Durant says, "We are what we repeatedly do. Excellence, then, is not an act, but a habit."

Learning how to connect with new people will have a huge impact in every area of your life. That's why it's so important to make socializing a part of your regular schedule.

If you're shy and you don't have a lot of experience meeting people, I can understand how this whole process could feel overwhelming.

This reminds me of Ivan, one of my previous coaching clients.

Ivan worked as a drafter for an engineering company and was terribly shy. He had bad social anxiety and easily got overwhelmed when there were too many people around him.

Even though he was good-looking and made a decent living, he barely had friends and didn't have a lot of success with his romantic relationships.

When we started working together, I asked him how often he went out. He said he barely did because he thought his only option was to go to bars and clubs, which he absolutely hated.

During the coaching program, I helped him find venues that aligned with his core values. This made socializing way more enjoyable for him.

Last time we chatted, he'd made some good friends and now actively goes on dates with women he's interested in.

I'm about to share with you exactly how he did it.

Here's how you put it all together.

Tip #1: Plan Ahead

Do a bit of research online and figure out the activities you're going to partake in. If you're not sure where to start, refer to the list in the last chapter of recommendations for good places to meet more like-minded people.

I suggest you plan out your calendar for the week on Sunday afternoon.

As a reminder, make sure to go to places and events you enjoy and that also have the kind of people you meet. It's hard to mingle while doing something that's not fun for you.

My recommendation is to go out at least three times a week. That's the minimum time you should invest socializing to see noticeable results.

Being busy is not an excuse. If this is important to you, you'll make it a priority.

Tip #2: Make It a Routine

Another thing you can do is look at your schedule and figure out how to integrate regularly meeting new people.

For example, I read books and worked from my laptop at trendy coffee shops as often as I could. I signed up for group fitness classes and regularly attended personal development seminars.

I do those things because it benefits me and because I know that the people I want to meet also go to those places.

Whatever you do, avoid doing things that isolate you. Limit playing video games and watching television as much as you can.

Tip #3: Only Do One Thing

Everybody will have different starting points in their journey to build a quality network.

No matter where you're at, only consume information that you need to learn at any given moment. Take action and get results before moving on to the next thing.

For example, if you're a total beginner, just focus on getting out of the house and doing more social things. If you're a bit more intermediate, start approaching more and more people. If you're more advanced, work on your humor and add some flirting in your conversation whenever you can.

The key here is to prioritize your learning and stay focused on the task at hand so you don't feel overwhelmed.

Follow these things if you want to meet the right people without wasting your time and money.

Chapter 13

The Fastest Way to Grow Your Network

Your network is the fuel that accelerates your success.

You'll not only benefit from learning useful knowledge from the individuals you meet, but also have access to their resources.

Before I tell you how, let me just remind of you something very important.

Your network is just a group of people who know, like, and trust you. It's about building genuine relationships, not exchanging business cards. Aspire to be your most authentic self in every situation.

Learn to approach people with a sense of curiosity by asking them about their family, their lives, and their hobbies and interests, not just their work. You want to treat every single person you meet like a friend, not just another contact. That's how you get to know people and create a deeper connection.

If you want to rapidly grow your network, simply introduce people who can benefit from each other.

When's the last time you had someone really listen to your struggles and come back with a solution to help you out?

The most recent example that comes to mind is when I launched my podcast. I'd been wanting to do it for the longest time, but I just had no idea where to even begin.

I mentioned this to a friend, and a few days later, I got an email introduction to someone who successfully launched his podcast.

After a couple more weeks of back and forth and getting my questions answered, I finally figured it out and got my podcast out there.

Today, I have tens and thousands of downloads from listeners all over the world and have connected with some of the biggest names in my industry. What a dream come true!

All of that became possible because of a simple email introduction. How much do you think I like that friend of mine? He's helped me out so much, so I'd be more than happy to return the favor when he needs it.

This strategy sounds so simple, but it's something most people fail to implement.

If you've ever met someone who's done this for you the same way I have, then you've met a super-connector.

Do you want to know how to become one?

Here's what I suggest.

Tip #1: Identify Someone's Need

Think of the people in your immediate network. What problems do they have?

If you're not sure, simply ask them. It's a good way to reconnect with old acquaintances and see what they've been up to as well.

You can either send an email or text asking how they're doing, what they're working on, and where they're getting stuck.

Tip #2: Find Someone with a Solution

After you've gotten a few responses, think of people in your network who would be able to help out. People always trust their friends' recommendations.

Have an abundance mentality and don't keep tabs on people. Give freely with no attachment to the outcome.

Tip #3: Make the Introduction

Once you've identified someone in need and someone who can help them, connect them. A simple email would do, or if possible, organize an in-person meeting.

Be a good host by mentioning a few interesting things about both people. This gives them something to work with to start off the conversation.

Introducing people in your network who could benefit from each other is a great way to add value to your existing relationships. Do this as much as you can and you'll be the first to come to mind when other people in your social circle think of an opportunity that could also benefit you.

Remember, if you help enough people get what they want, you'll eventually get what you want.

Chapter 14
How to Live a Life That Excites You

Throughout this book, you've heard me talk about the importance of finding your passion.

This is an absolute must if you want to become a person of value.

There's probably nothing more fulfilling than spending every single day of your life in a way that matters to you.

This is how you live a life by design, not default.

Going to a job you hate is hard. Living your life the way you want it is hard, too. My question to you is, which one would you rather struggle for?

When I realized this, I immediately put in my two-week notice and quit my high-paying engineering job. I can't go through another day doing something that I don't enjoy.

When I told my parents what I did, they thought I was crazy, but I didn't care. I was determined to change my situation.

I did what I had to do to make ends meet. I downsized my life, sold what I didn't need, and worked many odd jobs to make ends meet. I spent every other waking moment figuring out what my next steps were.

Was it hard? Of course. Was it worth it? Absolutely.

Now look, I'm not telling you to quit your job like I did. What I'm trying to say is, you have to be willing to do whatever it takes to live in alignment with your purpose.

Nowadays, going to bed is the worst part of my day. I get to do the things I want, when I want, and with whom I want.

Finding your passion is by far one of the most important things you can do for yourself.

If you're tired of living your life in quiet desperation, you have to do something about it.

Not sure where to start?

Here are seven questions you need to ask yourself to point you in the right direction.

1. What are topics and interests you love to learn about?

2. What are activities that you're naturally good at?

3. Who do you admire and look up to? Why?

4. If money wasn't an issue, what's something you would do?

5. Who do you love helping most? Why?

6. What are things other people rely on you for?

7. At the end of your life, how would you like to be remembered?

Take the time to answer these questions. This will serve as a roadmap for you to follow.

Once you have a few things figured out, start acting right away.

Look at your network and find someone who's already doing something you want to do. Take them out for lunch or coffee and listen to what they have to say.

Also, start educating yourself by reading books and listening to audiobooks and podcasts. We live in a time when you can learn almost anything you want. You just need to put in some time and effort.

That's exactly what I did, and it helped me immensely when I was just starting out. It took me a few years of sacrifice and hard work, but what's that compared to living in mediocrity your entire life?

You already have the answers within you. You just have to actually listen to it and do something about it.

Your goal is to do things that will make every single day of your life your perfect day.

Chapter 15
How to Become a People Magnet

It's been a few years now since I made a decision to do something about my social awkwardness.

Back then, I was staying at home and basically just watching way more television than any human should. I had been trying to go out and meet new people, but I found it extremely difficult.

Things didn't seem to click, and I was getting more and more frustrated because I didn't see any results. After going through countless rejections and lots of embarrassing moments, I decided to take a break and look at my situation differently.

I realized that I was focusing on the wrong things. Instead of always chasing after people, I wanted to find out how to become someone worth getting to know and to become magnetic.

That's when I made a conscious choice to improve the relationship with myself first.

I made a commitment to do more things that made me truly happy.

I started meditating more and visualizing every morning. I went to the gym regularly and ate healthier food. I focused on dressing well and grooming myself better. I read interesting books and started traveling more often.

Basically, I took the time to get to know who I really am, do more things that I wanted, and enjoy my own company.

After a while, I started to feel comfortable being alone. I didn't feel the need to chase after people anymore.

When I started going out to socialize again, I noticed something was different. Almost everyone I talked to responded to me more favorably.

I was a bit shocked because that rarely used to happen to me before.

At that moment, I learned a very important lesson. The biggest reason why people started treating me well was because I started treating myself well.

I improved my relationship with other people by focusing on myself first.

Fast-forward to today and I have more confidence, more dates, and more friends. I also have a bigger network full of more influencers than I could ever imagine.

Succeeding socially is simple: you attract exactly who you are.

Once you've identified what kind of people you want to have in your life, cultivate the same traits and qualities within yourself as well.

Not many people really talk about this because it's not easy. It takes a lot of hard work. But if you want long-lasting results, it's not only the best way to get there; it's the only way to get there.

Treat yourself like the most important person in your life, because you are. Everything else will sort itself out.

And that's how you become a people magnet.

Final Thoughts

Having the ability to turn a stranger into a friend has impacted every aspect of my life. I wrote this book to share with you the important lessons I've learned to build a network full of quality relationships.

At this point, you now have a plan to create a world-class social circle. If you implement the tips I share in this book, I can assure you that you'll succeed socially.

Regardless of your situation, start where you are and do what you can. Pick the smallest action you can take and implement it consistently. Eventually, it'll add up to something big, and that's how your life will change.

Remember, everything takes time and nothing great happens overnight.

Although you have the exact same system I use and teach my clients to build a network, you may be someone who wants to get to reach their goals a lot faster.

If that sounds like you, you might be a good fit for my coaching program. You'll get direct help from me and more specific feedback about your own situation.

The program will walk you through everything you need to learn to go from shy to social.

Go to the link below and book your free consultation. You'll just have to take a moment to answer a few questions. It'll give me a good idea where you're at and what you're looking to achieve.

Once I receive it, I'll get back to you as soon as I can.

>>> Go to

www.socialconfidencemastery.com/consultation

Whether we work together or not, send me a message anyway.

I love hearing from my readers. Let me know how you're doing and if there's anything I can help with you regarding your social confidence.

You can reach me at

info@socialconfidencemastery.com.

Here's to your social success,

Myke Macapinlac

Your Next Step

I'm confident that you now have the plan to improve your social confidence.

But here's the thing.

In order to take the next step, you need to know how to apply this to your day-to-day life.

That's why I created a cheat sheet that will help you approach and talk to anybody no matter how shy you are.

>>> Go to

www.socialconfidencemastery.com/cheatsheet

Inside, you will learn how to do the following:

- change your mindset by training your mind to improve the way you see yourself

- create a killer first impression and become a more likable person right away

- overcome social anxiety by building your courage to approach anybody you want to meet

- improve your conversation skills by learning how to tell good stories that captivate people

- design your ideal lifestyle by doing more of what you love while connecting with like-minded people

… and much, much more.

Check Out My Other Books

Would you like to learn how to improve your confidence, charisma, and social skills?

If so, I've written other books that will make you successful in all your social interactions.

>>> Go to www.socialconfidencemastery.com/books

You'll improve your social skills faster, meet the type of people you want to meet, and build the lifestyle you've always dreamed of.

Take action today and get this part of your life handled once and for all.

Can You Do Me a Favor?

Thanks for checking out my book.

I'm confident you will improve your social confidence if you follow what's written inside. But before you go, I have one small favor to ask.

Would you take 60 seconds and write a quick blurb about this book on Amazon?

Reviews are the best way for independent authors (like me) to get noticed, sell more books, and spread their messages to as many people as possible.

I also read every review and use the feedback to write future revisions—and even future books.

Please manually navigate to the book's page on Amazon in order to leave a review.

Thank you—I really appreciate your support.

About the Author

Myke Macapinlac was a shy immigrant who used to work a boring engineering job and became a talk show host, a social dynamics specialist, and a lifestyle entrepreneur.

He now teaches shy guys to develop social confidence so they can succeed in their personal, romantic, and professional lives.

His work has been featured in the *Calgary Herald*, on *Breakfast Television*, on Shaw TV, and in the *Huffington Post*.

To get to know him personally, visit his website at www.socialconfidencemastery.com

Printed in Great Britain
by Amazon